THE

FOOTBALL LEGENDS QUIZ

500+ CHALLENGING ALL-STAR TRIVIA QUESTIONS

BY

SEBASTIAN CARPENTER

Eaglestar Books

First published by Eaglestar Books, 2020

This Continental Edition first issued by Eaglestar Books in paperback and digital edition

Printed in Great Britain

Eaglestar Books

PO Box 7086

Harrow, London

HA2 5WN, United Kingdom

To all of the players and staff, past and present, who have worked for and dedicated themselves to the success of the beautiful game.

Contents

Preface

Football is the number 1 sport in the world. It has an estimated 3.5 billion fans worldwide, and according to FIFA's most recent Big Count survey, there are 265 million players actively involved in football around the world.

A.C Milan and Italian legend Andrea Pirlo stated that "Football is played with your head. Your legs are just the tools". This premise led to the creation of this publication as it is essential to have knowledge of the history and legends of the game past and present.

Re-live and test your knowledge of the most memorable moments from the FIFA World Cup, UEFA Euros, Copa América, Africa Cup of Nations, UEFA Champions League, English Premier League, La Liga, Serie A and many more!

The book contains questions and assesses your expertise on football facts, goals, domestic and international players, tournaments, trivia, trophies, transfers, and memorable occasions from over the years. In addition, endless fan-favourite players feature, such as: Pelé, Diego Maradona, Bobby Charlton, Franz Beckenbauer, Marco van Basten, Roberto Baggio, Romário, Paolo Maldini, Zinedine Zidane, Ronaldo, Ronaldinho, Lionel Messi and Cristiano Ronaldo to name but just a few.

Guaranteed fun is what awaits you as you'll be deep diving your brain to answer the 500+ quizzes that greet you in the pages that follow. The answers are included after every set of fifteen questions for your convenience. Be sure to keep an eye on your family members, friends or that guy from down the pub who may be scouring Google for the answers.

The game grips cities, countries, people and yourself. That's the power of the beautiful game. It's fun to play, watch and talk about with your friends, family and practically anybody. The passion is the No. 1 reason why football is the biggest and best sport on planet Earth.

Enjoy the book!

"To see the ball, to run after it, makes me the happiest man in the world."

Diego Maradona

"Without football, my life is worth nothing."

Cristiano Ronaldo

"Everything I have achieved in football is due to playing football in the streets with my friends."

Zinedine Zidane

"I learned all about life with a ball at my feet."

Ronaldinho

Round 1: Football Legends

1. Which player transferred to Real Madrid, in a world record deal at the time, for €77.5 million in 2001?

2. Nicknamed *Der Kaiser* ("The Emperor"), which former West German footballer won the FIFA World Cup as both a player in 1974, and as a manager in 1990?

3. How many English Premier League titles did Cristiano Ronaldo win with Manchester United?

4. Who led his country to the final of the 1974 FIFA World Cup and received the Golden Ball as player of the tournament?

5. Despite finishing in second place, which player became the first defender ever shortlisted for the FIFA World Player of the Year award in 1995?

6. On the 7th September 1956, Pelé scored on his debut as a 15-year-old in a 7-1 victory. Which club was he playing for?

7. At the age of 17, Ronaldo was called up to the Brazil squad for the 1994 FIFA World Cup, but he didn't play in any games. Which club did he choose to sign for after the tournament?

8. Which goalscoring machine was awarded the Ballon d'Or in 1965?

9. On the 5th July 1984, who was welcomed to his new club by 75,000 fans during an unveiling presentation at the Stadio San Paolo?

10. Born in Utrecht, Netherlands, which 1992 FIFA World Player of the Year winner had to retire from football prematurely at the age of 28?

11. Lionel Messi won the Olympic gold soccer medal with Argentina at which event?

12. On the 20th May 2007, which player scored his 1000th goal in a Vasco da Gama shirt against Sport Recife?

13. Staged at Hampden Park, Glasgow, the 1960 European Cup Final saw Real Madrid demolish Eintracht Frankfurt 7-3. Which player bagged a hat-trick for Madrid?

14. Which player was in England's 1966 FIFA World Cup Winning team, and the same year also picked up the Ballon d'Or?

15. Although he was Italy's stand-out performer at the 1994 FIFA World Cup, which player missed the decisive penalty against Brazil in the final?

Round 1 Answers

1. Zinedine Zidane.

2. Franz Beckenbauer.

3. Three titles (2006-07, 2007-08 and 2008-09).

4. Johan Cruyff.

5. Paolo Maldini.

6. Santos.

7. PSV Eindhoven.

8. Eusébio.

9. Diego Maradona.

10. Marco van Basten.

11. Beijing 2008 Summer Olympics.

12. Romário.

13. Alfredo Di Stéfano.

14. Bobby Charlton.

15. Roberto Baggio.

Round 2: Managers

16. Which manager led Aberdeen to success over Real Madrid in the 1983 European Super Cup Winners' Cup Final?

17. Louis van Gaal began his managerial career at which club?

18. Who was in charge of the Republic of Ireland from 2008 to 2013?

19. On the 22nd September 1996, Arsène Wenger was appointed manager at Arsenal. Who was fired to make way for Wenger?

20. Who had two spells at Bayern Munich spanning from 1998 to 2008, and won five Bundesliga titles during his tenure?

21. Which player, who later became manager, has made the most appearances for Arsenal in all competitions? He played in a record 722 games for the club.

22. The 2010 FIFA World Cup saw which manager lead Spain to glory in the final?

23. Celtic were guided to an unbelievable nine successive Scottish League titles between 1966 and 1974 by whom?

24. In his playing career, for which club did Brian Clough make the most appearances?

25. When Milan beat Real Marid 4-0 in the final of the 1993-94 UEFA Champions League, who was in charge?

26. Who left Huddersfield Town to become Liverpool manager in December 1959?

27. Which manager became the first to win the European Cup with an English team?

28. How many Bundesliga titles did Jürgen Klopp win at Borussia Dortmund?

29. In which city was Diego Simeone born?

30. Who managed the Ivory Coast at the 2010 FIFA World Cup in South Africa?

Round 2 Answers

16.   Sir Alex Ferguson.

17.   Ajax.

18.   Giovanni Trapattoni.

19.   Bruce Rioch.

20.   Ottmar Hitzfeld.

21.   David O'Leary.

22.   Vicente Del Bosque.

23.   Jock Stein.

24.   Middlesbrough.

25.   Fabio Capello.

26.   Bill Shankly.

27.   Sir Matt Busby.

28.   Two (2010-11 and 2011-12).

29.   Buenos Aires, Argentina.

30.   Sven-Göran Eriksson.

Round 3: Player Nicknames

31. Givanildo Vieira de Sousa is better known as whom?

32. When Paul Ince arrived at Manchester United, he requested that he would be called by the same nickname he had at West Ham United. What is it?

33. Who goes by the nickname of "El Matador"?

34. Real Madrid became known as the "Galácticos" for their purchasing of superstars during the presidency of whom?

35. Which ex-footballer is known as "The Romford Pelé"?

36. Javier Hernández is known in Spanish as "Chicharito", but what does it mean in English?

37. Plagued by injury, which player was known as "Sicknote" in the 1990s?

38. Famous for his acrobatic reflex saves, which goalkeeper was known as the "Black Spider" or "Black Panther"?

39. Ray Wilkins went by what nickname?

40. Gary Megson and which other manager have been labelled "The Ginger Mourinho"?

41. What did fans dub French striker Nicholas Anelka as?

42. "El Ángel Gabriel" was a nickname given to which former Fiorentina player and goalscoring strongman?

43. Which ex-footballer, who was a legend at Lazio and Juventus, was called "Furia Ceca" ("Czech Fury")?

44. Chelsea gave the nickname "Dave" to which Spaniard?

45. Who was called "Calamity" after a number of high-profile gaffes?

Round 3 Answers

31. "Hulk".

32. "The Guv'nor".

33. Edinson Cavani.

34. Florentino Pérez.

35. Ray Parlour.

36. "Little Pea".

37. Darren Anderton.

38. Lev Yashin.

39. "Butch".

40. Sean Dyche.

41. "Le Sulk".

42. Gabriel Batistuta.

43. Pavel Nedvěd.

44. Cesar Aspilicueta.

45. David James.

Round 4: Goalkeepers

46. At the 2002 FIFA World Cup, who became the first goalkeeper in the tournament's history to be awarded the Golden Ball?

47. Jens Lehmann joined Arsenal in 2003 replacing David Seaman. Which team did Lehmann join from?

48. Who was in goal for Brazil's 1994 FIFA World Cup winning team?

49. Where did Thibaut Courtois begin his playing career?

50. Hugo Lloris joined Tottenham Hotspur from which club in August 2012?

51. Before switching to Milan in May 1999, who was famous as a penalty-kick saving specialist whilst playing for Cruzeiro and Corinthians?

52. Which keeper won the First Division Championship, two European Cups, a UEFA Super Cup, and the Football League Cup whilst playing for Nottingham Forest?

53. David Ospina joined Arsenal from Nice in July 2014. Which country does Ospina represent at international level?

54. Who is the first goalkeeper to win the Serie A Footballer of the Year award?

55. David Seaman was signed for £1.3 million in 1990, which was a British record for a goalkeeper at the time. Which club did Arsenal buy him from?

56. How many FIFA World Cup's has Iker Casillias played in for Spain?

57.   Who won 92 caps between 1982 and 1998 playing for Wales?

58.   Which goalkeeper scored 41 goals overall and reportedly invented the "Scorpion Kick", a move that he executed perfectly to clear a cross from Jamie Redknapp in a friendly against England at Wembley in 1995?

59.   Where did Manchester United sign Peter Schmeichel from in August 1991?

60.   Who was the starting goalkeeper for the Italian side that finished third in the 1990 FIFA World Cup?

Round 4 Answers

46. Oliver Kahn.

47. Borussia Dortmund.

48. Cláudio Taffarel.

49. Genk.

50. Lyon.

51. Dida.

52. Peter Shilton.

53. Colombia.

54. Gianluigi Buffon.

55. Queens Park Rangers.

56. Four (2002, 2006, 2010 and 2014).

57. Neville Southall.

58. René Higuita.

59. Brøndby.

60. Walter Zenga.

Round 5: Defenders

61. After over 400 appearances for Lazio and Milan, which 2006 FIFA World Cup winner saw out his career at the MLS team Montreal Impact and then for Chennaiyin F.C. of the Indian Super League?

62. Jaap Stam retired from professional football in October 2007, which club was he playing for?

63. Who made his full international debut for France in March 2013 and was nominated for the Best Young Player award at the 2014 FIFA Word Cup?

64. Philipp Lahm spent the majority of his career at which club?

65. Marcel Desailly was born in which country?

66. Roberto Carlos left Inter Milan in 1996 because he wanted to play as a left back, but the manager wanted him to play as a winger. Who was the manager of Inter at this time?

67. In September 2017, who announced his desire to train and start boxing professionally?

68. Chelsea signed Kurt Zouma from which club in January 2014?

69. Who was awarded Man of the Match in Liverpool's 2018-19 UEFA Champions League victory over Tottenham Hotspur?

70. Who has played the most FIFA World Cup matches for Mexico with nineteen games under his belt?

71. Defender Joël Matip represents which country at international level?

72. The first footballer to win the BBC Sports Personality of the Year was in 1966. Who won it?

73. Which former Inter Milan star holds the most appearances for a foreign player tag in Serie A with 615 games?

74. Who did Real Madrid sign from Sevilla in the summer of 2005?

75. Where did Arsenal sign Steve Bould from in 1988?

Round 5 Answers

61. Alessandro Nesta.

62. Ajax.

63. Raphaël Varane.

64. Bayern Munich.

65. Accra, Ghana.

66. Roy Hodgson.

67. Rio Ferdinand.

68. AS Saint-Étienne.

69. Virgil van Dijk.

70. Rafael Márquez.

71. Cameroon.

72. Bobby Moore.

73. Javier Zanetti.

74. Sergio Ramos.

75. Stoke City.

Round 6: Midfielders

76. Which player scored the only goal of the game in the 2019-20 UEFA Champions League Final?

77. Who won the 2018 Ballon D'or?

78. How many English Premier League titles did David Silva win with Manchester City?

79. Which manager of Rangers signed a 19-year-old Gennaro Gattuso from Perugia in July 1997?

80. Al Saad of Qatar hired which former Barcelona legend as their manager in May 2019?

81. Who coached the Japanese team to victory in the 2004 Asian Cup and led them to the 2006 FIFA World Cup in Germany?

82. How many goals did Cristiano Ronaldo score in the 2016-17 UEFA Champions League victory over Juventus?

83. Who is the only player to have scored and be on the winning team in an FA Cup Final, a League Cup Final, a UEFA Cup Final, and a UEFA Champions League Final?

84. Which team did Chelsea loan Kevin de Bruyne out to in July 2012?

85. Roy Keane began his professional playing career at which club?

86. How many European Cups did Graeme Souness win with Liverpool?

87. Michel Platini came out of retirement in November 1988 and completed an unusual feat at international level by

representing two nations. Who was he playing for in the friendly against the Soviet Union?

88. Who spent four years as Scotland captain and two seasons as Leeds United captain?

89. The 2018 Footballer of the Year award in Germany was won by which player?

90. What squad number did Patrick Vieira wear for Arsenal between 1996 and 2005?

Round 6 Answers

76.   Kingsley Coman.

77.   Luka Modrić.

78.   Four (2011-12, 2013-14, 2017-18 and 2018-19).

79.   Walter Smith.

80.   Xavi.

81.   Zico.

82.   Two.

83.   Steven Gerrard.

84.   Werder Bremen.

85.   Cobh Ramblers.

86.   Three (1977-78, 1980-81 and 1983-84).

87.   Kuwait.

88.   Gary McAllister

89.   Tony Kroos.

90.   No. 4.

Round 7: Forwards

91. Who began his professional playing career at Al Mokawloon in 2010?

92. Which Italian scored his only competitive goal for Chelsea in a 1-1 draw at Liverpool in 1998?

93. The 2013 FIFA Puskás Award for the "most beautiful goal" after a stunning bicycle kick during an international match, was presented to whom?

94. Who is the Netherland's all-time top scorer with 50 goals?

95. Which prolific striker did A.C. Milan sign from Chelsea in June 1961?

96. The Golden Boot given by the English Premier League has been won on four separate occasions by which player?

97. In 2018, George Weah became the President of which nation?

98. Which striker joined Liverpool from Real Madrid in January 2005?

99. Brazil beat Germany 2-0 in the 2002 FIFA World Cup Final with two goals from which player?

100. Which striker won the African Player of the Year a record four times?

101. Slavia Prague's all-time leading goal scorer is whom?

102. Who won the Golden Boot at the 1996 UEFA European Championships with five goals?

103. Playing in Japan with Vissel Kobe as of 2019, who is Spain's all-time top goal scorer?

104. On the 5th September 2012, who became the highest -paid footballer to ever play in Australia after signing with Sydney FC?

105. In August 2014, Liverpool signed Mario Balotelli for £16 million as a replacement for Luis Suárez. Which team did Liverpool buy Balotelli from?

Round 7 Answers

91. Mohamed Salah.

92. Pierluigi Casiraghi.

93. Zlatan Ibrahimović.

94. Robin van Persie.

95. Jimmy Greaves.

96. Thierry Henry.

97. Liberia.

98. Fernando Morientes.

99. Ronaldo.

100. Samuel Eto'o.

101. Josef Bican.

102. Alan Shearer.

103. David Villa.

104. Alessandro Del Piero.

105. A.C. Milan.

Round 8: Amazing Goals

106. Roberto Carlos scored a spectacular free kick in a 1-1 draw against France at the start of which tournament?

107. David Beckham sent England to the 2002 FIFA World Cup with a late free kick against Greece. But what was the final score in the match?

108. Name the player that scored an overhead kick for Liverpool in a 1-0 victory over Watford in May 2017? This goal later received the BBC Goal of the Season award.

109. Frank Lampard scored a chip against Barcelona at the Camp Nou during a UEFA Champions League encounter in 2006. How did the match finish?

110. Gianfranco Zola scored his amazing back-flick goal in a 4-0 win for Chelsea against which side back in 2002?

111. In March 2005, which team did Ronaldinho score a toe-poke against in the UEFA Champions League round-of-sixteen?

112. Which goalkeeper did Diego Maradona score the "Goal of the Century" against?

113. Marco van Basten scored a wonderful volley in the Netherland's 2-0 victory over the Soviet Union in the UEFA Euro 1988 Final. Which player scored the other goal?

114. In June 2001, Rivaldo scored an overhead kick for Barcelona which propelled them into the Champions League. They won the match 3-2, who was it against though?

115. Name the Liverpool player that hit a thunderous left-footed strike from a free kick in a 3-1 win against Manchester United? This shot flew into the top corner leaving the United goalkeeper Fabien Barthez completely helpless.

116. Which Liverpool striker completed his hat-trick against Norwich City with an incredible 45-yard strike at Carrow Road? The game finished 3-0 to Liverpool and was played in April 2012.

117. Who won the 2019-20 Premier League Goal of the Season for his wonderful individual effort against Burnley?

118. How old was Michael Owen when he went on a solo run that led to that excellent goal at the 1998 FIFA World Cup against Argentina?

119. Andros Townsend won the 2018-19 Premier League Goal of the Season in Crystal Palace's 2-1 victory over which club?

120. Tony Yeboah scored two unforgettable goals for Leeds United in the 1995-96 Premier League season. Name the two teams he scored these legendary goals against?

Round 8 Answers

106. 1997 Tournoi de France.

107. 2-2.

108. Emre Can.

109. 2-2.

110. Norwich City.

111. Chelsea.

112. Peter Shilton.

113. Ruud Gullit.

114. Valencia.

115. John Arne Riise.

116. Luis Suárez.

117. Son Heung-min.

118. 18-years-old.

119. Manchester City.

120. Liverpool and Wimbledon.

Round 9: Finals

121. Who did Algeria beat 1-0 to win the 2019 African Cup of Nations?

122. The post-war FIFA World Cup of 1950 saw which country beat Brazil 2-1 in the final?

123. Aston Villa beat Bayern Munich 1-0 in the 1982 European Cup Final, who scored the only goal of the game?

124. From 1976 to 1982, an English team won the European Cup every year. Which teams won it during this period?

125. When did Brazil win the World Cup for the first time?

126. The 2013 UEFA Europa League Final saw Chelsea beat which club?

127. Who scored the only goal of the game in Liverpool's 1-0 victory over Flamengo in the 2019 FIFA Club World Cup Final?

128. Which city hosted the 2017 UEFA Champions League Final?

129. Manchester United beat Crystal Palace 2-1 in the 2016 FA Cup Final. Who scored for United?

130. Colombia beat Mexico 1-0 in the 2001 Copa América Final. Which former Inter Milan legend scored for Colombia?

131. Sevilla were demolished 5-0 in the 2018 Copa del Ray Final by which team?

132. Which country won the 2019 AFC Asian Cup?

133. The 2003 FIFA Confederations Cup Final was played out by France and Cameroon. France won the match 1-0, who scored for them?

134. Who did Fulham beat 2-1 in the 2019-20 EFL Championship Promotion Play-offs Final?

135. Who did Liverpool defeat 2-0 in the 2003 League Cup Final?

Round 9 Answers

121. Senegal.

122. Uruguay.

123. Peter Withe.

124. Liverpool, Nottingham Forest and Aston Villa.

125. 1958 FIFA World Cup, Sweden.

126. Benfica.

127. Roberto Firmino.

128. Millenium Stadium, Cardiff.

129. Juan Mata and Jesse Lingard.

130. Iván Córdoba.

131. Barcelona.

132. Qatar.

133. Thierry Henry.

134. Brentford.

135. Manchester United.

Round 10: Stadiums

136. On the 16th July 1950, Uruguay beat Brazil 2-1 in the final match of the FIFA World Cup. Which stadium did the match take place in?

137. Where do Bradford City play their home matches?

138. The Stadio Artemio Franchi is home to which football club?

139. Inter Milan beat Bayern Munich 2-1 in the 2009-10 UEFA Champions League Final. Where was it held?

140. Galatasaray S.K. play at which stadium?

141. Spain's 4-0 victory over Italy in the UEFA Euro 2012 Final was played at which stadium?

142. Where do Paris Saint Germain play their home matches?

143. What is the capacity at the Camp Nou?

144. Estadio Monumental Antonio Vespucio Liberti is home to which Argentinian team?

145. Argentina beat West Germany 3-2 in the 1986 Fifa World Cup Final. Where did the final take place?

146. LA Galaxy play their home matches at which stadium?

147. What year did the new Wembley Stadium open its doors?

148. Where do the Republic of Ireland play their home matches?

149. The Estádio do Dragão is home to which club?

150. Liverpool are one of the few teams that successfully managed to defend the European Cup. They achieved this in 1978 by winning the competition again, having done so the previous year. Which stadium hosted the 1978 European Cup final?

Round 10 Answers

136.   Maracanã Stadium, Rio de Janeiro.

137.   Valley Parade.

138.   Fiorentina.

139.   Santiago Bernabéu Stadium, Madrid.

140.   Türk Telekom Stadium, Istanbul.

141.   Olympic Stadium, Kiev.

142.   Le Parc des Princes, Paris.

143.   99,354.

144.   River Plate.

145.   Estadio Azteca, Mexico City.

146.   Dignity Health Sports Park, Los Angeles.

147.   2007.

148.   Aviva Stadium (Lansdowne Road), Dublin.

149.   FC Porto.

150.   Wembley, London.

Round 11: Club Nicknames

151. "The Yellow Submarine" ("El Submarino Amarillo") is the nickname of which club?

152. What was Chelsea's old nickname?

153. The Italian national team are known as what?

154. Celtic go by what nickname?

155. "Bafana Bafana" was coined as a nickname by the fans of which country?

156. Which set of fans gave their club the nickname "Los Millonarios" ("The Millionaires")?

157. Crystal Palace are nicknamed what?

158. What are the Australian national team known as?

159. Which nation are called the "Taeguk Warriors"?

160. This African country are dubbed the "Super Eagles". Who is it?

161. Which Argentinian team goes by the name of "La Leprosos" ("The Lepers")?

162. Who are the "Tractor Boys"?

163. The nickname of the Welsh football team is what?

164. This South American national team is known as "La Roja" ("The Reds") in Spanish. Who is it?

165. What is the nickname of Peterborough United?

Round 11 Answers

151. Villareal.

152. "The Pensioners".

153. "The Azzurri".

154. "The Bhoys".

155. South Africa.

156. River Plate.

157. "The Eagles".

158. Socceroos.

159. South Korea.

160. Nigeria.

161. Newell's Old Boys.

162. Ipswich Town.

163. "The Dragons".

164. Chile.

165. "Posh".

Round 12: Transfers

166. Who became the first ever Brazilian to sign for Arsenal in 1999?

167. Where did Leicester City sign Riyad Mahrez from in January 2014?

168. In July 2000, who made a surprise move from Barcelona to their rivals Real Madrid which set a new world record fee at the time?

169. Ian Wright signed for Arsenal in a deal worth £2.5 million in September 1991. Which team did they sign him from?

170. Which player was signed by Chelsea from Internacional in July 2012?

171. On the 4th July 2013, who moved from Saint-Étienne to Borussia Dortmund on a five-year contract?

172. Who became the first British footballer sold for £1 million in 1979? He moved from Birmingham City to Nottingham Forest.

173. Jack Grealish was loaned out from Aston Villa to which club in September 2013?

174. Which team did Liverpool sell Kevin Keegan to in the summer of 1977?

175. Jordan Henderson signed for Liverpool in June 2011. Which club did Henderson sign from?

176. At the age of 19, Javier Saviola joined Barcelona from which club in 2001?

177. In May 2013, which player was signed by Barcelona from Santos?

178. Who did Juventus sign from Napoli for a fee of €90 million in July 2016?

179. On the 23rd January 2019, which player did Barcelona announce would be joining them from Ajax on a five-year contract?

180. Davor Šuker joined Arsenal for the 1999-00 season. Which club did he sign from?

Round 12 Answers

166.   Sylvinho.

167.   Le Havre.

168.   Luís Figo.

169.   Crystal Palace.

170.   Oscar.

171.   Pierre-Emerick Aubameyang.

172.   Trevor Francis.

173.   Notts County.

174.   Hamburger SV.

175.   Sunderland.

176.   River Plate.

177.   Neymar.

178.   Gonzalo Higuaín.

179.   Frenkie de Jong.

180.   Real Madrid.

Round 13: Logos

181. The Roman myth of Romulus and Remus, feature on which club's crest?

182. Which Italian club have a rooster on their badge?

183. One team in the English Premier League has a cannon on their badge, which team is it?

184. What do Leicester City have on their logo?

185. Everton have which tower on their badge?

186. The diamond on Villareal's logo is which two colours?

187. How many bulls are there on FC Red Bull Salzburg's emblem?

188. Botafago have what on their badge?

189. What is on West Bromwich Albion's logo?

190. The ball on the Barcelona emblem is what colour?

191. The stripe on Real Madrid's badge is which colour?

192. What colours are Eintracht Frankfurt's logo?

193. How many stars are there on Aston Villa's badge?

194. What do Sydney F.C. have on their emblem?

195. Which South American outfit celebrate a famous Portuguese explorer on their crest by exhibiting a sailboat?

Round 13 Answers

181.   Roma.

182.   S.S.C. Bari.

183.   Arsenal.

184.   A fox.

185.   Prince Rupert's Tower.

186.   Red and yellow.

187.   Two bulls.

188.   A white star.

189.   A hawthorn.

190.   Gold.

191.   Blue.

192.   Red and white.

193.   One star.

194.   Sydney Opera House.

195.   Vasco da Gama.

Round 14: Captains

196. Who captained England from 1996 to 2000?

197. After inheriting the club captaincy from Aldair in October 1998, who became Serie A's youngest ever captain?

198. Raúl claimed the Real Madrid captaincy in June 2002, but who was his predecessor?

199. Which player was captain when Brazil won the 2002 FIFA World Cup?

200. Who was Manchester United's captain when they defeated Benfica in the 1968 European Cup Final?

201. Initially behind Frank de Boer and Michael Reiziger in the Barcelona pecking order, which shaggy haired individual went on to captain the club from 2004 to 2014.

202. Who was France's skipper throughout the 1998 FIFA World Cup success?

203. What year did Roy Keane take over the Manchester United captaincy from Eric Cantona?

204. Which player captained Arsenal in both the 2015 and 2017 FA Cup final victories?

205. AC Milan's captain for 15 years, later known as "Kaiser Franz", is whom?

206. Fernandinho became the Manchester City captain for the 2020-21 season; but who was selected as the vice-captain?

207. Who was captain of Bayern Munich from 2002 to 2008?

208. Tottenham Hotspur became the first team in the 20th century to complete the double. Who captained them to this success?

209. After John Terry left Chelsea in 2017, who was appointed as the new captain?

210. Who was Arsenal captain when the team became 'The Invincibles' in the 2003-04 season?

Round 14 Answers

196. Alan Shearer.

197. Francesco Totti.

198. Fernando Hierro.

199. Cafu.

200. Bobby Charlton.

201. Carles Puyol.

202. Didier Deschamps.

203. 1997.

204. Per Mertesacker.

205. Franco Baresi.

206. Kevin De Bruyne.

207. Oliver Kahn.

208. Danny Branchflower.

209. Gary Cahill.

210. Patrick Vieira.

Round 15: Defenders 2nd Round

211. What nationality is defender Stig Inge Bjørnebye?

212. Whilst playing in Italy, Taribo West made the most appearances for which club?

213. How many league titles did Alan Hansen win with Liverpool?

214. Cristian Romero plays internationally for which country?

215. Which team did Robin Le Normand sign for in July 2016?

216. Pepe was born in which country?

217. Achraf Hakimi signed for which club in July 2020?

218. Claudio Gentile spent the bulk of his career at which club?

219. On the 10th May 2016, which defender re-joined Bayern Munich on a five-year contract?

220. Thiago Silva played for AC Milan between 2009 to 2012. How many Serie A titles did he win?

221. The former Coventry and Liverpool defender Phil Babb earned 35 caps playing for which country?

222. Neil Ruddock joined Liverpool in 1993 from Tottenham Hotspur. What is Ruddock's nickname?

223. Séamus Coleman began his career at which Irish club?

224. Daniel Passarella played for which two Serie A teams?

225. Jérôme Boateng represents which country at international level?

Round 15 Answers

211. Norwegian.

212. Inter Milan.

213. Eight titles.

214. Argentina.

215. Real Sociedad.

216. Brazil.

217. Inter Milan.

218. Juventus.

219. Mats Hummels.

220. One (2010-11).

221. Republic of Ireland.

222. "Razor".

223. Sligo Rovers.

224. Fiorentina and Inter Milan.

225. Germany.

Round 16: Midfielders 2nd Round

226. Who became the manager of Juventus in August 2020?

227. Which player did Real Madrid loan to Porto in July 2014?

228. The first Croatian to score in a FIFA World Cup final was whom?

229. How many English Premier League titles did Paul Scholes win with Manchester United?

230. Marco Verratti represents which country at international level?

231. In January 2009, Jordan Henderson joined which Championship club on loan for one month?

232. Jan Mølby won three league titles during his time at Liverpool. Which club was the Danish footballer signed from?

233. Which former Villareal man won the Argentine Footballer of the Year four times?

234. With his distinctive hairstyle, who is Colombia's most capped player?

235. Romanian fans gave which ex-footballer the nickname "Regele" ("The King")?

236. In July 2008, Philippe Coutinho was purchased by Inter Milan from Vasco da Gama. How old was he?

237. Ex-Barcelona man, Phillip Cocu managed which club from 2013 to 2018?

238. In 2009, Ariel Ortega had a stint in Turkey with which club?

239.   Which Danish footballer was included in the 2017-18 PFA Team of the Year?

240.   After playing for Germany in the 1998 FIFA World Cup, which club did Dietmar Hamman join for a fee of £5.5 million.

Round 16 Answers

226.   Andrea Pirlo.

227.   Casemiro.

228.   Ivan Perišić.

229.   Eleven (1995-96, 1996-97, 1998-99, 1999-00, 2000-01, 2002-03, 2006-07, 2007-08, 2008-09, 2010-11 and 2012-13).

230.   Italy.

231.   Coventry City.

232.   Ajax.

233.   Juan Román Riquelme.

234.   Carlos Valderrama.

235.   Gheorghe Hagi.

236.   16-years-old.

237.   PSV.

238.   Fenerbahçe S.K.

239.   Christian Eriksen.

240.   Newcastle United.

Round 17: Forwards 2nd Round

241. Which Norwegian won the Austrian Bundesliga and Austrian Cup with FC Red Bull Salzburg in the 2019-20 season?

242. Who was the English Premier League's top scorer in the 2015-16 and 2016-17 seasons?

243. This Belgian scored 49 goals in 101 matches for Aston Villa in all competitions. Who is he?

244. Andriy Shevchenko saw out his career with which club?

245. Miroslav Klose won two Bundesliga titles in the 2007-08 and 2009-10 seasons, which club was he playing for?

246. The Premier League Golden Boot was won for the first time by a non-European in the 1998-99 season. Who won the award?

247. Which Frenchman scored the match-winning goal against Spain in the 2010 UEFA European Under-19 Championship?

248. Three players shared the Golden Boot award in the 2018-19 season, each scoring 22 goals. Pierre-Emerick Aubameyang was one of the players, along with two Liverpool players. Who were the two Liverpool forwards?

249. In March 2012, who became the first African player to score 100 Premier League goals?

250. Which team signed Ciro Immobile in July 2016?

251. Which player won the 2016 Brazilian Player of the Year award as Palmeiras won their first national league title in twenty-two years? He moved to the English Premier League in 2017.

252. Name the striker that was signed by Rafael Benítez from Blackburn Rovers in the summer of 2006?

253. The golden goal in the UEFA Euro 2000 Final between France and Italy was scored by which player?

254. Which German won the Silver Ball at the 2014 FIFA World Cup?

255. The 2011, 2012, and 2014 French Player of the Year awards went to whom?

Round 17 Answers

241. Erling Haaland.

242. Harry Kane.

243. Christian Benteke.

244. Dynamo Kyiv.

245. Bayern Munich.

246. Dwight Yorke.

247. Alexandre Lacazette.

248. Mohamed Salah and Sadio Mané.

249. Didier Drogba.

250. S.S. Lazio.

251. Gabriel Jesus.

252. Craig Bellamy.

253. David Trezeguet.

254. Thomas Müller.

255. Karim Benzema.

Round 18: Kit Sponsors

256.   Who were Manchester United's sponsor when Carlos Tevez joined in August 2007?

257.   During the 1997 to 1999 campaigns, who sponsored Fiorentina?

258.   PlayStation 2 sponsored which French club from 1998 to 2007?

259.   From 2000 to 2003, when the likes of Mark Viduka, Harry Kewell and Alan Smith played for Leeds United, which sponsor did they don on their shirts?

260.   Who sponsored Rangers from 1987 to 1999?

261.   As of the 2020-21 season, West Ham United are sponsored by whom?

262.   Which company started sponsoring Juventus in 2012?

263.   On the 1st May 1986, Diego Maradona played one game for Tottenham Hotspur against Inter Milan. Who sponsored Spurs at the time?

264.   When Gary Speed and Jay-Jay Okocha played for Bolton Wanderers, who sponsored their kits?

265.   Which team are sponsored by Ideal Boilers in the 2020-21 FA Premier League campaign?

266.   Who sponsored Liverpool before Carlsberg?

267.   Inter Milan have a long-standing relationship with which sponsor?

268. West Ham United's shirt was sponsored by who from 1998 to 2003?

269. Who sponsors Valencia's 2020-21 jersey?

270. From 1988 to 2000, who sponsored Parma?

Round 18 Answers

256. AIG.

257. Nintendo.

258. Auxerre.

259. Strongbow.

260. McEwan's Lager.

261. Betway.

262. Jeep.

263. Holsten Pils.

264. Reebok.

265. West Bromwich Albion.

266. Candy.

267. Pirelli.

268. Dr. Martens.

269. Bwin.

270. Parmalat.

Round 19: Transfers 2nd Round

271. In March 2017, Bastian Schweinsteiger left Manchester United to join which club?

272. Which Dutchman did Real Madrid sign from Sampdoria in 1996?

273. In the summer of 1994, who moved from AS Monaco to Tottenham Hotspur for a fee of £2 million?

274. On the 5th October 2020, Justin Kluivert joined RB Leipzig on loan from which club?

275. Where did Sheffield Wednesday sign Paolo Di Canio from in August 1997?

276. Jamie Redknapp was signed by Liverpool in January 1991, at the age of 17. Which club did Liverpool sign him from?

277. Which club did Real Madrid sign Robinho from in July 2005?

278. Which team did Chelsea sign Timo Werner from? He signed for £47.5 million in June 2020.

279. What year did Real Madrid sign Steve McManaman from Liverpool?

280. Gary McAllister signed for Leicester City in 1985 from which Scottish club?

281. In July 2009, Obafemi Martins left Newcastle United for which team?

282. Where did Real Madrid sign Marcelo from in January 2007?

283. Dani Alvez joined Barcelona in July 2008 from which club?

284.   On the 30th June 2008, who signed for Chelsea from
        Barcelona on a three-year contract?

285.   Sami Hyypiä was signed by Liverpool in May 1999 for £2.6
        million. Where did he sign him from?

Round 19 Answers

271. Chicago Fire.
272. Clarence Seedorf.
273. Jürgen Klinsmann.
274. AS Roma.
275. Celtic.
276. AFC Bournemouth.
277. Santos.
278. RB Leipzig.
279. 1999.
280. Motherwell.
281. VfL Wolfsburg.
282. Fluminense.
283. Sevilla.
284. Deco.
285. Willem II.

Round 20: Nationalities

286. The former Liverpool player Igor Bišćan represented which country at international level?

287. Sadio Mané played for which country at the 2012 Summer Olympics in London?

288. An ex-captain of the Swedish national team, who retired after Euro 2012 after amassing 117 caps for his country?

289. What is André Ayew's country of birth?

290. Hristo Stoichkov netted 37 times for which country?

291. In which city was Salomón Rondón born?

292. In 2013, Mariano Díaz played and scored in a friendly match for which country?

293. Where is Mustapha Hadji from?

294. Arsenal signed club legend Cliff Bastin in 1929. Bastin went on to score 178 goals for Arsenal and helped the club win five league titles. Which team was Bastin represent at international level?

295. David Alaba made his debut as a nineteen-year-old in 2009 for which country?

296. Jay-Jay Okocha played as an attacking midfielder for which country?

297. Which country does Gary Medel captain?

298. Where is Artem Dzyuba from?

299. Edin Džeko plays internationally for which country?

300. Ex-Parma and Roma star Hidetoshi Nakata played 77 times for which country?

Round 20 Answers

286.   Croatia.

287.   Senegal.

288.   Olof Mellberg.

289.   France.

290.   Bulgaria.

291.   Caracas, Venezuela.

292.   Dominican Republic.

293.   Morocco.

294.   England.

295.   Austria.

296.   Nigeria.

297.   Chile.

298.   Russia.

299.   Bosnia and Herzegovina.

300.   Japan.

Round 21: English Premier League Set 1

301.   Which former Arsenal player admitted he threw a slice of pizza which hit Sir Alex Ferguson in the face? This occurred in the tunnel after Manchester United had ended Arsenal's long unbeaten run in October 2004.

302.   Who received a 9 month ban from football after doing a fly-kick at a fan in the crowd? The player had already been sent-off in the game.

303.   How many matches was Luis Suárez banned for after he bit Branislav Ivanović on the arm?

304.   Which player scored from his own half on the opening day of the 1996-97 campaign?

305.   A slip from Steven Gerrard proved costly for Liverpool's title challenge in the 2013-14 season. Which Chelsea player went on to score following Gerrard's slip?

306.   Which Manchester United footballer was sent off in their 4-1 home loss to Liverpool in March 2009?

307.   After scoring for Manchester City against his former club Arsenal, who ran the length of the pitch to celebrate in front of his former team's fans?

308.   Who is the only Welsh player to win the PFA Players' Player of the Year award on two occasions?

309.   Which Manchester City player scored a pivotal goal from outside the box to seal an important 1-0 victory over Leicester City on the 6th May 2019? This helped Manchester City to win the title six days later.

310.   How many times did Cristiano Ronaldo win the PFA Players' Player of the Year award?

311. Where did Leeds United sign Mark Viduka from?

312. How many Premier League clubs did David Ginola play for?

313. Who is Portsmouth's all-time leading goal scorer in the Premier League?

314. Patrik Berger was signed by Liverpool from which German club in August 1996?

315. Pierre van Hooijdonk played for which Premier League team?

Round 21 Answers

301. Cesc Fàbregas.

302. Eric Cantona.

303. Ten matches.

304. David Beckham.

305. Demba Ba.

306. Nemanja Vidić.

307. Emmanuel Adebayor.

308. Gareth Bale.

309. Vincent Kompany.

310. Two times (2006-07 and 2007-08).

311. Celtic.

312. Four (Newcastle United, Tottenham Hotspur, Aston Villa and Everton).

313. Aiyegbeni Yakubu.

314. Borussia Dortmund.

315. Nottingham Forest.

Round 22: English Premier League Set 2

316. Which player is Southampton's all-time leading goal scorer in the Premier League?

317. Where did Chelsea sign Arjen Robben from for £12.1 million in 2004?

318. Damien Duff moved to which Australian club after leaving Fulham?

319. Manchester United signed a left back from Monaco who went on to make over 250 league appearances for them and win 5 Premier League titles. Who is this player?

320. Arsenal signed Patrick Vieira for £3.5 million in August 1996. Name the club that sold him to Arsenal?

321. How many times did Juninho sign on loan or permanently for Middlesbrough?

322. Thierry Henry wore which squad number on his shirt for his whole first stint at Arsenal?

323. Name the four Premier League clubs that Michael Owen played for?

324. Which two Premier League teams did both Michael Duberry and Jimmy Floyd Hasselbaink play for?

325. Which squad number did Dwight Yorke wear on his shirt at Manchester United?

326. Name the only two players to win Premier League titles with both Arsenal and Manchester City?

327. Which Jamaican international won the Premier League with Leicester City in 2015-16?

328. Romelu Lukaku played on loan for which two Premier League teams?

329. Carlos Tevez and Javier Mascherano joined West Ham in the summer of 2006. Name the club that sold the two players to West Ham?

330. Which World Cup winner joined Birmingham City on loan in 2003?

Round 22 Answers

316. Matt Le Tissier.

317. PSV.

318. Melbourne City.

319. Patrice Evra.

320. A.C. Milan.

321. Three times (1995, 1999 and 2002).

322. Number 14.

323. Liverpool, Newcastle United, Manchester United and Stoke City.

324. Leeds United and Chelsea.

325. Number 19.

326. Kolo Touré and Gaël Clichy.

327. Wes Morgan.

328. West Bromwich Albion and Everton.

329. Corinthians.

330. Christoph Duggary.

Round 23: English Premier League Set 3

331. Which two Premier League teams has Daniel Sturridge played for on loan?

332. Robbie Keane was loaned out by Inter Milan to a Premier League club in December 2000. Name the club he joined on loan?

333. Which Spanish player did Everton sign on loan from Real Sociedad in January 2005?

334. George Weah signed on loan for which team in January 2000?

335. The Ghanaian international, Asamoah Gyan was signed by a Premier League outfit for £13 million from Rennes in August 2010. Which club signed him?

336. Which Premier League club did Danny Welbeck join on loan in August 2010?

337. Who scored the 25,000th goal in the Premier League?

338. One Premier League goalkeeper kept a record 24 clean sheets in just one season. Name the goalkeeper?

339. Who scored the first Premier League hat-trick?

340. Which goalkeeper holds the record of 14 consecutive games without conceding a goal?

341. Who are the two players to win the Golden Boot with one team and then successfully defend the Golden Boot after transferring to another club?

342. Name the only two players to have won the Ballon d'Or whilst playing for a Premier League club?

343. Which player scored the most goals in a single game after coming on as a substitute? He scored a record 4 goals after coming on the pitch.

344. Who scored the 10,000th goal in the Premier League whilst playing for Tottenham Hotspur?

345. This Blackburn Rovers player scored the 5,000th goal in the Premier League, who is it?

Round 23 Answers

331. Bolton Wanderers and West Bromwich Albion.

332. Leeds United.

333. Mikel Arteta.

334. Chelsea.

335. Sunderland.

336. Sunderland.

337. Zlatan Ibrahimović.

338. Petr Čech.

339. Eric Cantona.

340. Edwin van der Saar.

341. Alan Shearer and Robin van Persie.

342. Michael Owen and Cristiano Ronaldo.

343. Ole Gunnar Solskjær.

344. Les Ferdinand.

345. Chris Sutton.

Round 24: English Premier League Set 4

346. Virgil van Dijk's first club in the Premier League was Southampton. But where did Southampton sign the Dutch international from?

347. Fernando Torres signed for Liverpool in July 2007. Which team did Liverpool purchase him from?

348. Which three players from the Premier League played in the 1998 FIFA World Cup Final?

349. Who finished as the top goal scorer in the UEFA Euro 2004?

350. Name the four Premier League players who were on the winning team in the 2018 FIFA World Cup final?

351. Who is the top scoring Costa Rican player in Premier League history?

352. Which two clubs did Ugo Ehiogu play for?

353. Who is top scorer from the country of Mali in the Premier League?

354. John Carew played for which two teams in the Premier League?

355. Nigel Martyn made 372 appearances in the Premier League. Which three teams did he play for?

356. Who is the top scoring Finnish player in Premier League history?

357. Joe Cole made a total of 378 appearances in the Premier League. Name the four teams that he played for?

358. Who is the only Serbian to have scored a hat-trick in the Premier League?

359. In December 2000, which player received a standing ovation at Goodison Park after catching a cross into the opponent's penalty box with his hands when the Everton goalkeeper was injured?

360. Who is the top scoring Jamaican player in Premier League history?

Round 24 Answers

346.   Celtic.

347.   Atlético Madrid.

348.   Frank Leboeuf, Emmanuel Petit and Patrick Vieira.

349.   Milan Baroš.

350.   Hugo Lloris, N'Golo Kanté, Paul Pogba and Olivier Giroud.

351.   Paolo Wanchope.

352.   Aston Villa and Middlesbrough.

353.   Frédéric Kanouté.

354.   Aston Villa and Stoke City.

355.   Crystal Palace, Leeds United and Everton.

356.   Mikael Forssell.

357.   West Ham United, Chelsea, Liverpool and Aston Villa.

358.   Savo Milošević.

359.   Paolo Di Canio.

360.   Jason Euell.

Round 25: English Premier League Set 5

361. Who was the first Italian to play in the Premier League?

362. Which Honduran left back scored from his own half for Wigan Athletic against Stoke City?

363. Blackburn Rovers won the Premier League title in the 1994-95 season, who was their captain?

364. Which player scored a hat-trick in Middlesbrough's 8-1 victory against Manchester City in May 2008?

365. Louis Saha made his first Premier League appearance for which team?

366. Who was the first midfielder in the Premier League to score 100 goals?

367. Which player has scored a hat-trick for three different Premier League teams?

368. This player tops the stats for the most assists with 162, who is it?

369. The first ever Premier League goal was scored by whom?

370. Which two players have scored a Premier League hat-trick by using only their heads?

371. Who secured Arsenal's 2001/02 title win with an away goal against Manchester United at Old Trafford?

372. The top goal scorer in the very first Premier League season was whom?

373. Which player scored the 20,000th Premier League goal?

374. He scored five goals in one-half of a match in the Premier League, who is he?

375. The fastest ever goal in the Premier League was scored in just 7.69 seconds. Who scored it?

Round 25 Answers

361.   Andrea Silenzi.

362.   Maynor Figueroa.

363.   Tim Sherwood.

364.   Alfonso Alvez.

365.   Newcastle United.

366.   Matt Le Tissier.

367.   Nicholas Anelka.

368.   Ryan Giggs.

369.   Brian Deane.

370.   Duncan Ferguson and Salomón Rondón.

371.   Sylvain Wiltord.

372.   Teddy Sheringham.

373.   Mark Albrighton.

374.   Jermaine Defoe.

375.   Shane Long.

376. Which player has made the most consecutive appearances in the Premier League with a total amount of 310?

377. In January 2001, which Colombian striker signed for Aston Villa from River Plate for £9.5 million?

378. Who provided the assist to Sergio Agüero's injury time title-winning goal against QPR in the 2011-12 campaign?

379. Which player holds the record for the most Premier League appearances with 653 games?

380. The record for consecutive goals scored in a game by one player currently stands at 11 games, who set it?

381. Which defender set the record for the most expensive British transfer at that time after switching from Leeds United to Manchester United in July 2002?

382. Two Newcastle United players were famously sent off for fighting each other in a game against Aston Villa. Who are the two players?

383. Which Egyptian switched to from FC Basel to Chelsea in January 2014?

384. How old was Wayne Rooney when he moved from Everton to Manchester United?

385. Who was the first goalkeeper to score a goal in the Premier League?

386. Which South African legend captained Leeds United?

387. One defender scored 22 penalties, which is a record for a Premier League defender. Name the player?

388. Which Argentinian broke British transfer records at the time following a £28.1 million move in July 2001?

389. Bryan Roy used to play for which Premier League team?

390. How many times did Ruud van Nistelrooy win the Golden Boot award?

Round 26 Answers

376. Brad Friedel.

377. Juan Pablo Ángel.

378. Mario Balotelli.

379. Gareth Barry.

380. Jamie Vardy.

381. Rio Ferdinand.

382. Lee Bowyer and Kieron Dyer.

383. Mohamed Salah.

384. 18-years-old.

385. Peter Schmeichel.

386. Lucas Radebe.

387. David Unsworth.

388. Juan Sebastián Verón.

389. Nottingham Forest.

390. One time (2002-03).

Round 27: FIFA World Cup Set 1

391.   The FIFA World Cup has been won the most times by which nation?

392.   Who scored a hat-trick for England in their 1966 FIFA World Cup victory over West Germany?

393.   How many times have Argentina won the World Cup?

394.   Which two European countries have contested a final a piece but have never won the competition?

395.   Who was the first European country to win a World Cup?

396.   How many times have Uruguay won the World Cup?

397.   Which player has won the World Cup on three occasions?

398.   The record for the most appearances at the World Cup stands at 25 games. Which German achieved this feat?

399.   Which Turk scored the fastest ever goal ever at a World Cup against South Korea in just 10.89 second?

400.   Who is the oldest player to score a goal at a World Cup? He was 42 years and 39 days old.

401.   The youngest player to score at a World Cup was 17 years and 239 days old. Who was it?

402.   Name the player who scored the fastest ever brace in World Cup history? He did this in a 2014 FIFA World Cup semi-final.

403.   Which player has received a record seven yellow cards in the competition? The player in question is from Argentina.

404. Two goalkeepers hold the joint-record for keeping 10 clean sheets in the World Cup. One is from England and the other is from France. Who are they?

405. Which Brazilian player holds the record for coming on 11 times as a substitute at the World Cup?

Round 27 Answers

391. Brazil (1958, 1962, 1970, 1994 and 2002).

392. Geoff Hurst.

393. Two times (1978 and 1986).

394. Sweden and Croatia.

395. Italy (1934).

396. Two times (1930 and 1950).

397. Pelé (1958, 1962 and 1970).

398. Lothar Matthäus.

399. Hakan Şükür.

400. Roger Milla.

401. Pelé.

402. Toni Kroos.

403. Javier Mascherano.

404. Peter Shilton and Fabien Barthez.

405. Denílson.

Round 28: FIFA World Cup Set 2

406. Which Croatian scored the only own goal to date in a World Cup Final?

407. The only 0-0 in a World Cup final by which two countries?

408. How many times have France won the World Cup?

409. Where will the 2022 FIFA World Cup be staged?

410. Which two countries held a joint World Cup?

411. The first African nation to hold a World Cup was which country?

412. How many times has Cafu won the World Cup with Brazil?

413. Which two countries have been losing finalists whilst hosting the competition?

414. Where was the 1962 FIFA World Cup held?

415. The final of the 1994 FIFA World Cup was played at which stadium?

416. What year did Switzerland host the World Cup?

417. Name the five countries that have hosted the World Cup on two occasions?

418. Jan Jongbloed made appearances in consecutive finals for which team?

419. Who was in goal for Italy in the 1994 FIFA World Cup Final?

420. Who was in goal for Brazil when they conceded 7 goals to Germany in the 2014 FIFA World Cup?

Round 28 Answers

406. Mario Mandžukić.

407. Brazil vs. Italy (1994 FIFA World Cup Final).

408. Two times (1998 and 2018).

409. Qatar.

410. South Korea and Japan (2002 FIFA World Cup).

411. South Africa (2010 FIFA World Cup).

412. Two times (1994 and 2002).

413. Brazil (1950) and Sweden (1958).

414. Chile.

415. Rose Bowl, Los Angeles.

416. 1954.

417. Brazil, Mexico, France, Germany and Italy.

418. Netherlands.

419. Gianluca Pagliuca.

420. Júlio César.

Round 29: FIFA World Cup Set 3

421. Which defender received the Silver Ball Award for his outstanding performances at the 2006 FIFA World Cup?

422. Name the French defender that was sent off in the 1998 FIFA World Cup final?

423. Uruguay's captain at the 2018 FIFA World Cup was whom?

424. Who score for Italy in the 2006 FIFA World Cup Final?

425. Which player was the captain for Germany when they won the 1974 FIFA World Cup?

426. How many times have Italy won the World Cup?

427. Which England defender had a headed goal disallowed in the round of 16 tie against Argentina at the 1998 FIFA World Cup?

428. The Golden Boot at the 2014 FIFA World Cup was picked up by whom?

429. Which Brazilian winger won Player of the Tournament at the 1962 FIFA World Cup?

430. Germany's midfield maestro at the 2002 FIFA World Cup scored three goal on their way to the final. Who is he?

431. Who captained England at the 2010 FIFA World Cup?

432. Australia's top goal scorer in World Cup history is whom?

433. Zinedine Zidane scored two of France's three goals in the 1998 FIFA World Cup Final. Who scored the other goal for the French?

434. Name the midfielder who scored a penalty for the Netherlands in the 1974 FIFA World Cup final?

435. Which goalkeeper started the 2010 FIFA World Cup Final for the Netherlands?

Round 29 Answers

421. Fabio Cannavaro.

422. Marcel Desailly.

423. Diego Godlin.

424. Marco Materazzi.

425. Franz Beckenbauer.

426. Four times (1934, 1938, 1982 and 2006).

427. Sol Campbell.

428. James Rodriguez.

429. Garrincha.

430. Michael Ballack.

431. Steven Gerrard.

432. Tim Cahill.

433. Emmanuel Petit.

434. Johan Neeskens.

435. Maarten Stekelenburg.

Round 30: FIFA World Cup Set 4

436.   Who won the Golden Boot at the 1986 FIFA World Cup?

437.   Name the player that finished the 2002 FIFA World Cup as top goal scorer with eight goals?

438.   Denmark's all-time top goal scorer in World Cup history is whom?

439.   Which Brazilian striker started the final in both the 1994 and 1998 FIFA World Cups?

440.   Name the Italian player that finished the 1982 FIFA World Cup as the top goal scorer of the competition?

441.   Italy's two starting forwards in their 2006 FIFA World Cup Final victory was whom?

442.   Which German won the Golden Boot at the 1970 FIFA World Cup?

443.   Who captained the Argentina side in the 2014 FIFA World Cup final?

444.   Who was the manager of France when they exited the competition at the group stage in 2010? Behind the scenes they had lots of problems and the players even refused to train at one stage.

445.   Which manager famously sent Roy Keane home from 2002 FIFA World Cup?

446.   Name the manager that led England to two World Cup quarter finals in 2002 and 2006?

447.   Who was England's manager for their 1966 FIFA World Cup win?

448. Which country knocked the United States of America out of the competition when they were the hosts? This was in a round of 16 game at the 1994 FIFA World Cup.

449. Germany's manager at the 2002 FIFA World Cup was whom?

450. Who was Russia's captain when they hosted the competition in 2018?

Round 30 Answers

436. Gary Lineker.

437. Ronaldo.

438. John Dahl Tomasson.

439. Bebeto.

440. Paolo Rossi.

441. Francesco Totti and Luca Toni.

442. Gerd Müller.

443. Lionel Messi.

444. Raymond Domenech.

445. Mick McCarthy.

446. Sven-Göran Eriksson.

447. Sir Alf Ramsey.

448. Brazil.

449. Rudi Völler.

450. Igor Akinfeev.

451. South Africa only won one game when they hosted the competition in 2010. They exited the World Cup at the group stage, but who was their win against?

452. Who knocked Russia out of the 2018 FIFA World Cup? Russia lost at the quarter-final stage on penalties.

453. Which nation knocked the joint hosts Japan out of the 2002 FIFA World Cup in a second-round game?

454. Name the German player that scored a wonderful 30-yard strike against Costa Rica in the 2006 FIFA World Cup? He made it 4-2 to Germany with this strike after receiving a pass from a free kick.

455. Which Dutch player scored one of the goals of the 1998 FIFA World Cup in a game against Argentina? The player in question collected a 60-yard pass from Frank de Boer, touched it through a defender's legs and then volleyed into the goal with the outside of his right foot.

456. Name the Scottish player that scored a fantastic goal against the Netherlands at the 1978 FIFA World Cup? The footballer played a one-two with Kenny Dalglish before running into the area and scoring past the goalkeeper.

457. Which England player famously did a "salmon dive" towards the ball in his own penalty area in an attempt to stop his team conceding a goal at the 2010 FIFA World Cup against Slovenia?

458. The Brazilian player Rivaldo was involved in a controversial moment at the 2002 FIFA World Cup. A player on the opposing team kicked the ball at his thigh but Rivaldo pretended the ball hit him in the face and got the player sent off. Which team were Brazil playing against in this game?

459. Zinedine Zidane was sent off for a headbutt during the 2006 FIFA World Cup Final. Which Italian player did he headbutt?

460. David Beckham was sent off during a quarter final match at the 1998 FIFA World Cup for kicking out at a player. Which player did Beckham kick out at?

461. Which player emerged as one of the main stars of the 1990 FIFA World Cup? This player did a dance by the corner flag after scoring each goal.

462. Who has made the most appearances at the World Cup for Argentina?

463. Portugal's top-goal scorer at the World Cup overall is whom?

464. Which Argentinian player scored a hat-trick against South Korea at the 2010 FIFA World Cup?

465. Name the oldest player to score a hat-trick at a World Cup? He did this at 33 years and 130 days old. This was against Spain at the 2018 FIFA World Cup.

Round 31 Answers

451. France.

452. Croatia.

453. Turkey.

454. Torsten Frings.

455. Dennis Bergkamp.

456. Archie Gemmill.

457. John Terry.

458. Turkey.

459. Marco Materazzi.

460. Diego Simeone.

461. Roger Milla.

462. Diego Maradona.

463. Eusébio.

464. Gonzalo Higuaín.

465. Cristiano Ronaldo.

Round 32: UEFA Champions League Set 1

466. Which German team beat Legia Warsaw 8-4 in the 2016-17 UEFA Champions League group stages?

467. An English team has been involved in two 4-4 draws in the competition. One was with another English team and the other was against Ajax, who is it?

468. Which Ukrainian team has reached a Champions League semi-final?

469. Who took charge of a record 190 games in the Champions League?

470. Rafael Benítez won the Champions League with which club?

471. Who was the first player to reach the milestone of making 100 Champions League appearances?

472. Which player is the youngest to score a hat-trick on his Champions League debut? He did this at 18 years and 340 days old.

473. One player scored a hat-trick on his Champions League debut whilst playing for Newcastle United against Barcelona, who was it?

474. Who are the only brothers to have both scored a Champions League hat-trick?

475. Only one goalkeeper has been sent off in a UEFA Champions League Final. Who is that goalkeeper?

476. Who scored Manchester United's injury time winner against Bayern Munich in the 1999 UEFA Champions League Final?

477. In the 2004 UEFA Champions League Final, who played in goal for FC Porto?

478. Name the goalkeeper that started the 2019 UEFA Champions League Final as Tottenham Hotspur's captain?

479. Which Brazilian international was a losing finalist with Bayer 04 Leverkusen, but later went on to win the competition with Inter Milan?

480. Who is the youngest ever manager to win the competition at 38 years and 129 days old?

Round 32 Answers

466.   Borussia Dortmund.

467.   Chelsea.

468.   Dynamo Kyiv.

469.   Sir Alex Ferguson.

470.   Liverpool.

471.   Raúl.

472.   Wayne Rooney.

473.   Faustino Asprilla.

474.   Filippo and Simeone Inzaghi.

475.   Jens Lehmann.

476.   Ole Gunnar Solskjær.

477.   Vítor Baía.

478.   Hugo Lloris.

479.   Lúcio.

480.   Pep Guardiola.

481. Ashley Cole has played for which three teams in the UEFA Champions League?

482. Which French defender won the Champions League with both Marseille and A.C. Milan?

483. This Brazilian midfielder finished top goal scorer in the competition for the 2006-07 season, who is he?

484. Deco won the UEFA Champions League with which two teams?

485. Which Czech Republic midfielder missed the 2003 UEFA Champions League Final through suspension? At the time he played for Juventus.

486. Who was the first Englishman to win the UEFA Champions League with two different teams?

487. One striker was the top goal scorer in the competition in the 2003-04 season whilst on loan at Monaco. Who was he?

488. Name the player that scored two goals for A.C. Milan in the 2005 UEFA Champions League Final?

489. An Inter Milan striker scored two goals in the 2010 UEFA Champions League Final. Who was the player?

490. Which Barcelona forward opened the scoring in the 2011 UEFA Champions League Final?

491. Name the only English team to progress through the group stages after losing their opening three games?

492. Which Belgian team came from 3-0 down to draw 3-3-3 against Arsenal during the 2014-15 group stage?

493. Real Madrid won the home time of the 2004 quarter final 4-2. However, they went out on away goals after losing the away tie 3-1. Which team knocked them out?

494. Which Real Madrid player scored a left footed volley from a Roberto Carlos looping cross in the 2002 UEFA Champions League Final?

495. Which Bayern Munich player captained and scored for his team in the 2001 UEFA Champions League Final?

496. Name the Chelsea player that scored a tremendous left footed volley from outside the box against Barcelona? This was in the semi-final in the 2008-2009 season.

497. Who came on as a substitute and scored a sublime lob for Borussia Dortmund in the 1997 UEFA Champions League Final?

498. Leeds United reached the Champions League semi-final stage in the 2000-01 season. Who was their manager during this season?

499. Which Manchester United player scored a 40-yard strike against FC Porto in the 2009 knockout phase?

500. Who was Ajax's manager when they won the Champions League Final in 1995?

501. Which Valencia midfielder captained his side in both their Champions League Final defeats? He also scored in one of the finals.

Round 33 Answers

481.   Arsenal, Chelsea and Roma.

482.   Marcel Desailly.

483.   Kaká.

484.   FC Porto and Barcelona.

485.   Pavel Nedvěd.

486.   Owen Hargreaves.

487.   Fernado Morientes.

488.   Hernán Jorge Crespo.

489.   Diego Milito.

490.   Pedro.

491.   Newcastle United.

492.   Anderlecht.

493.   Monaco.

494.   Zinedine Zidane.

495.   Stefan Effenberg.

496.   Michael Essien.

497.   Lars Ricken.

498.   David O'Leary.

499.   Cristiano Ronaldo.

500.   Louis van Gaal.

501.   Gaizka Mendieta.

Congratulations!

You have completed all 33 rounds of The Football Legends Quiz Book.

One last thing

If you have enjoyed the quiz book, please write a review about this publication. This is helpful for the author and it will provide useful feedback.